635.986

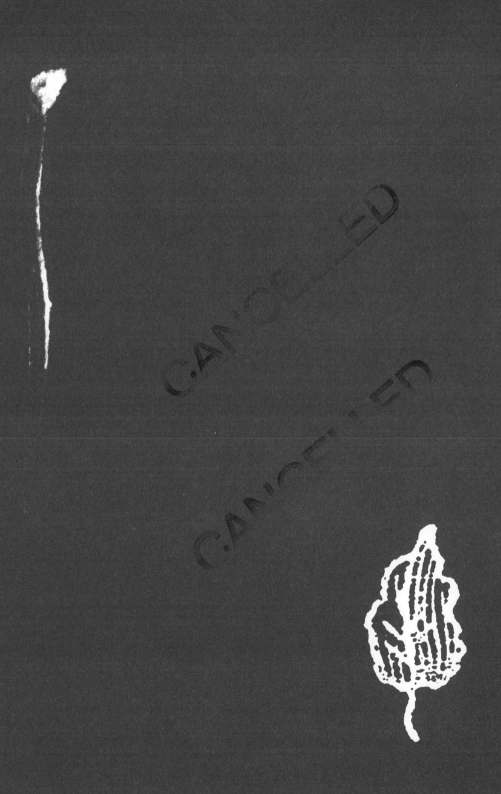

Christine Walkden's
no-nonsense
container
gardening

Christine Walkden's no-nonsense container gardening

The secret of growing vegetables, herbs, fruit and flowers in small spaces

SIMON &
SCHUSTER
ILLUSTRATED

London · New York · Sydney · Toronto · New Delhi

A CBS COMPANY

First published in Great Britain by Simon & Schuster
UK Ltd, 2013
A CBS COMPANY

SIMON & SCHUSTER
ILLUSTRATED BOOKS
Simon & Schuster UK Ltd
222 Gray's Inn Road
London
WC1X 8HB

www.simonandschuster.co.uk

Simon & Schuster Australia, Sydney

Simon & Schuster India, New Delhi

Commercial director: Ami Richards
Consultant editor: Francine Lawrence
Project editor: Sharon Amos
Designer: Miranda Harvey
Photography: Jacqui Hurst
Front cover and additional photography: Oskar Proctor
Photographic design consultant: Georgina Rhodes
Production manager: Katherine Thornton

A CIP catalogue record for this book is available from
the British Library

ISBN 978-0-85720-692-3

Printed and bound in China
Colour reproduction by Dot Gradations Ltd, UK

Notes
AGM refers to the Royal Horticultural Society's Award of Garden Merit
and denotes a variety of outstanding quality which will grow in all sorts
of soil types and conditions.
F1: An F1 hybrid is a plant that has been produced by cross-pollinating
two parent lines which have been selected for particular characteristics.

contents

first steps

We can all can find space to grow something in a container, whether it's a window box on the fourth floor, a hanging basket outside the front door, a pot by the back doorstep – even a growbag on top of a canal-boat cabin. Everyone can have a go at container growing, without having to have what most of us think we need – a garden.

Growing plants in containers means you can add a splash of colour where it's needed, rearrange pots to create different dramatic effects whenever you want to. It's the perfect way for beginners to get started before tackling bigger spaces and a great way to interest children too.

growing in containers

siting the container

Start by thinking about where you're going to position your containers. That'll help you decide what you need. Do you want pots that complement or contrast with their surroundings? You will, for example, need to take into account texture, shape and colour (see page 18).

Even when you do have a garden or small outdoor space, containers are still incredibly useful. You can use them to alert visitors to a change in level, by indicating the edge of a patio or a set of steps. Small pots can be lifted and moved to fill gaps in the border or to bring instant seasonal decor to windowsills; once that display is over, they're just as easily replanted with next season's plants.

Tubs of flowering plants make a lovely welcome at the front door (as opposite); this is one site where it's a good idea to go for really heavy containers, to make sure passersby think twice about trying to run off with them.

Take into account how sunny or shady a spot is and plant containers accordingly. Ferns and some evergreens will do fine in shade and brighten what might be a rather dark corner. Tough succulents such as sedums and sempervivens love baking heat and need very little maintenance. To get maximum enjoyment from your pots, put a garden seat nearby or make sure you can see them from a window.

Top: A pot of *Narcissus* 'Rip van Winkle' cheers up a windowsill in spring.
Above: Containers filled with geraniums lead the way to a well-stocked greenhouse.
Opposite: Densely packed tubs of tulips with the occasional hyacinth welcome visitors to the house.

scale and size

Think big! A large pot can make a dramatic statement even in a small space. But do your homework first. Make sure you're happy with the position of the container before you fill and plant it: a fully planted-up urn will be too heavy to shift without a barrow or trolley. This rule applies even to regular-size pots – rearrange containers until you're happy with the set-up *before* you start planting up. It's better for your back and the plant.

Match plant to pot as a general rule. A pansy will always look best in a small container while a tree or shrub needs a tall deep tub.

Beware of containers with a narrow top and a bulbous base as this makes repotting or replanting almost impossible once the plant gets too big for the container. Often the only answer is to break the pot. Bulbous pots may also split in the winter due to the pressure of water freezing while the narrow neck prevents expansion of the compost or soil.

There is a way round this: find a smaller pot that fits neatly inside the neck of the bulbous pot and plant this up instead, remembering to lift it out before winter. That's how the huge spherical terracotta pot (right) has been planted and it's also a clever juxtaposition of scale: the low frill of nasturtiums on top will soon start to trail over the sides. It's the exception that breaks the rule to matching size of plant to pot.

Top: An old tin can makes a hanging planter for summer verbena. **Above**: Nasturtiums will soon trail over this spectacular terracotta pot. **Opposite**: Huge oil cans salvaged from a restaurant are plenty big enough for beans, sweet peas and globe artichokes.

Overleaf: Pots of French marigolds in front of tomatoes are not only pretty but useful too, as they may help deter whitefly.

shape, colour and texture

There are two aspects to colour. One is aesthetic: do you want your container to contrast with or complement the overall background colour? A white container against a white wall will disappear, while a white container against a grey or blue wall will stand out. Matching a pot to the colour of a plant's flowers or leaves is a neat trick for a coordinated look.

The other is practical. White can soon become grubby and is difficult to keep clean. Black pots may look smarter but tend to absorb heat in a sunny position and may even 'cook' the plant's roots – though there are ways of preventing this problem (see page 34).

Now to shape. From voluptuously curvy terracotta to architectural linear concrete pots and everything in between, containers must be practical as well as beautiful to look at. A square-bottomed container is more stable than one with a round bottom – an important consideration if you are growing trees, as their height often makes them top heavy. Avoid shallow dish shapes for all but succulents and alpines: the soil can overheat in summer and dry out quickly; in winter it can easily freeze.

Texture can add charm, from the tactile rough surface of a weathered concrete urn to the shiny light-reflecting glaze of a colourful china pot and the dimpled pattern of moulded plastic.

the usual suspects

Good old terracotta has been around for hundreds of years and its natural warm brown colour makes it ideal for almost any situation. Terracotta pots come in all shapes and sizes, from the tiniest thumb pot to great Mediterranean urns and oil jars. Their porous nature keeps roots cool in summer – though this also means they are prone to drying out. Look for pots labelled frostproof if they are to stay out all year round. Glazed terracotta pots give you the option of colours other than brown.

Don't underestimate plastic, whether you choose imitation terracotta or funky coloured pots. Plastic is light to lift, cheap to buy and pots won't dry out so quickly in summer. But they become brittle with age and colour can fade.

Stone and reconstituted stone containers look fab but have one big drawback – their weight, not to mention price. They are long-lasting and keep plant roots insulated from extremes of temperature.

Other options to consider include wooden troughs and barrels, metal containers and short-lived fibre pots and planters.

Traditionally reserved for tomatoes, aubergines and other tender crops, growbags have moved out of the greenhouse and on to the patio thanks to decorative shallow troughs or willow edging, which disguise the bag.

Top: Plastic is fantastic – it's light, cheap and colourful. **Above**: Classic terracotta is unbeatable in the style stakes. **Opposite**: Gorgeous glazes extend your options when choosing terracotta.

'As long as it holds soil and has drainage holes, you can grow plants in practically anything'

beg, steal or borrow

There are really no restrictions on the types of containers you can use. The key thing to remember is that whatever you choose should have sufficient drainage holes – waterlogging is the most common cause of failure in container growing. Likewise, don't use anything too small and make sure containers are free from old soil, grease, oil and other contaminants. The only limitation is your imagination – and your budget.

In times of austerity and thriftiness, recycling comes into its own. I have seen wicker baskets, pretty tin cans, oil drums, colanders, plastic milk bottles, old packing cases, shopping baskets, Wellington boots, watering cans, wheelbarrows, zinc buckets, old tyres, willow containers, half-barrels, wooden crates, mangers and even builders' merchant bags, all planted up with equal success.

Just follow the advice on drainage, lining (where necessary) and type of compost in the next chapter to turn your recycled find into a perfect container for growing plants.

Top: Waste not want not. Wash out coffee cups and cans and use plastic cutlery for markers. **Above**: Button-sized cobweb sempervivums fit neatly into the holes in engineering bricks. **Opposite**: The drum from a washing machine makes a futuristic planter for grasses.

plan and
prepare

You've chosen your containers and now it's time to prepare them ready for planting up. The most important thing is that they should be clean. Old soil clinging to the sides may carry diseases that can infect new soil and crops or flowers. Get a bucket of hot soapy water and a stiff brush and scrub thoroughly.

This is a good time to sort out any drainage problems. You may need to make extra holes in unusual containers – turn to page 35 to find out how. The metal pot opposite is a vintage rubber-tapper's pot, used to collect latex from rubber trees, so it needed a few holes drilling.

Group containers in their final position before planting, to avoid shifting heavy pots.

get ready

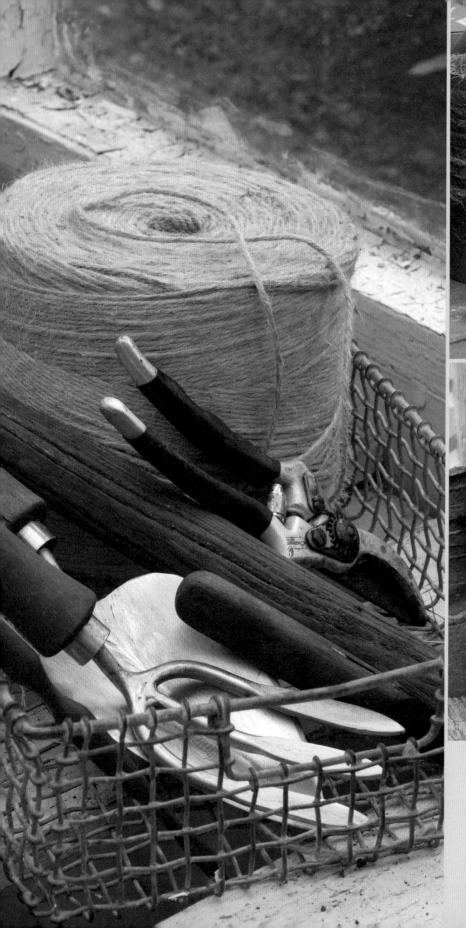

Left: Keep tools together in a handy wire basket. **Top**: Other paraphernalia that will be useful include gloves, shears, waterproof marker pens and labels, and bottles of liquid feed. **Above**: A stack of inverted rubber-tapper's pots and more conventional terracotta.

the tools you'll need

If you only have a small balcony or patio, then the chances are you probably don't have anywhere to store garden tools, so you'll need to keep them to a minimum. Some people manage with an old fork and spoon from the cutlery drawer – and, to be honest, you can make do if you have only a few pots. But you'll find container gardening easier with the right tools for the job. Most gardeners find that they have just three items they use all the time: a good trowel, a small fork and secateurs.

You will also need string or wire, scissors and a stiff brush for cleaning pots. You should be able to keep all your equipment in a nice trug, bucket or box – stand it by the patio doors or tuck it under a garden seat. Keep a bundle of bamboo canes in a corner and, of course, you'll need a watering can – these can look decorative in their own right standing at the ready next to a group of pots. Keep some horticultural fleece handy – you may need it for winter frost protection of tender plants or to keep pests off crops.

It's always wise to label pots and seedlings – you may think you'll be able to remember what's what but it's very easy to forget. Waterproof marker pens are best and you can endlessly reuse white plastic labels – or try using lolly sticks or even plastic cutlery.

Top: Wind garden twine round canes to create a wigwam for beans or sweet peas. Horticultural fleece protects from frost and pests. **Above**: Coir pots are naturally biodegradable; you can put them straight into the soil.

compost

There are basically two types of compost: soil-based and soilless. 'Soilless' types are mainly derived from organic matter – bark, sawdust, green waste, coir, coconut fibre, paper, leafmould – to which nutrients and water-retaining agents have been added.

The commonest soil-based compost is sold under the John Innes formula: some are produced specifically for container growing. The formula is based on loam, peat and sand, to which different amounts of fertiliser and lime are added. No. 2 is useful for containers, while No. 3 should be used for permanent plantings such as trees and shrubs.

I use soilless types for quick-growing crops or where the plants are only going to be in the pot or container for a year, and soil-based composts when I am planting trees or shrubs into containers.

Reusing compost

I am often asked if it's fine to use garden soil for filling containers and I always say no. The reason for this is that it may contain pests and diseases or weeds and often its drainage properties are not suitable for use in the confines of a pot.

The old saying that you get what you pay for holds true in the world of composts. The cheapest will contain few if any nutrients or water-holding materials, but may be okay for plants that will be growing in it for only a short time, such as lettuce.

Top: Carrots, onions and broad beans (to right of foreground) do well in multipurpose compost. **Above**: Open the bag up and roll down the top for easy access. **Opposite**: Get stuck in – it's lovely stuff!

Christine's tip

I always avoid buying the bottom five bags of compost on a pallet, as they have been subjected to the weight of all the other bags on top of them in the stack. In my experience plants grown in compost from these bags do not perform as well.

Top left: It's easy to drill drainage holes in metal containers. Always wear goggles to guard against flying shards of metal. **Middle left**: Add drainage in the form of broken up polystyrene: it's lightweight and you're bound to have some lying around. Metal heats up quickly in summer: several layers of newspaper will protect roots from extremes of temperature. **Bottom left**: Fill with compost. **Above**: The finished container planted with mint – an ideal candidate for a pot as it is invasive in garden beds.

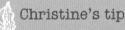 Christine's tip

Always add a barrier layer between the drainage materials and the compost, to stop the compost washing down and blocking drainage holes. Use old net curtains, washing-up cloths, pillowcases, capillary matting, sacking or landscape fabric, cut to the shape of the container.

the importance
of drainage

The most common reason for failure in container growing is lack of drainage. The majority of plants do not like sitting with their roots in water.

Ideally a container should have a decent-sized hole about 1cm (½in) in diameter every 15cm (6in) – more if you can get away with it. You'll invariably have to make more drainage holes in non-standard containers. To drill holes in stone and terracotta try my method: place a big blob of plasticine or Blu-Tack where you need a hole, then use a sharp masonry bit to drill through it into the container. The plasticine stops the stone or terracotta from shattering.

To drill plastic without splitting put adhesive tape on either side first – or use a hot spike to make holes. Drill tin and other metals direct but wear goggles.

If the container cannot be drilled, half-fill it with drainage material and do not overwater.

Drainage material
My general rule is to fill the container to at least a third of its depth with drainage material. Use crocks – broken clay pots – placed curved-side uppermost to prevent them collecting stagnant water; gravel or chippings; polystyrene left over from packaging; even rubble and broken bricks in large containers.

Above: Don't waste broken pots – they still have a useful life as drainage crocks in the bottom of containers.

growing plants from seed

Growing plants from seed is satisfying and exciting and doesn't need a lot of equipment. You can do most things on the kitchen table: in fact, it's a good place to begin, as some ornamental plants and half-hardy vegetables need to be started off under cover. Tomatoes, runner beans, cucumbers, sweetcorn and courgettes, for example, would all be killed by frost if sown outdoors before May. You don't need a greenhouse to do this: I raise all the seeds on my dining-room table and windowsills.

First bring the compost into the house the night before: cold compost can slow down germination. Cover the table with polythene to protect it.

It's easier to sow larger seeds such as runner beans in individual pots. Fill the pots with compost and firm it down using a small tamper or the base of another pot before pushing in a single seed.

To water, either soak the pots in a washing-up bowl of lukewarm water for a couple of hours or use a very fine rose on the end of a watering can.

Sowing in trays
Overfill the seed tray and then remove the surplus compost to leave a level surface: I use a firming board that fits the seed tray exactly – I made my own but you can buy them. Firm it down further so the seed tray is three-quarters full and then scatter the seed on top.

Above: There are always more seeds in a packet than you need. Store any surplus in packets, in an airtight container, in the salad drawer of the fridge. Or, even better, do a seed swap with friends and neighbours. **Opposite**: A small dibber is useful for making holes for large seeds such as beans, to the recommended depth on the packet – but I just use my finger! Sow beans individually after tamping down the compost, water well and label.

more sowing techniques

Don't sow the whole packet if you need only a few plants. Sowing too thickly can result in damping-off, a fungal disease, which can kill all of your seedlings. Always read the packet: not all seeds need to be covered with compost, and doing so may stop them growing altogether. If you do need to cover them, use a fine sieve and cover to the recommended depth. Firm this covering very gently to ensure seeds are in contact with the compost and that the surface is level.

Most seeds will germinate and come through in 2–3 weeks. Keep the trays moist but not wet. Once the seedlings are at a size you can handle easily, they need to be 'pricked out' to give each room to grow.

Pricking out

Water the seedlings the day before you want to prick them out. Fill a seed tray with multipurpose compost and level it. Carefully prise the seedlings out of the tray, keeping as much compost round the roots as possible. Replant in the new tray, spacing them in rows so that there is about 3–5cm (1¼–2in) between plants. Or replant the seedlings into individual pots.

Hardening off

Once the plants are about 6–8cm (2¼–3in) tall, start to harden them off. Do this over 2–3 weeks. Take the plants outside for a few hours each day, gradually increasing the length of time. After a couple of weeks, they will be ready for planting out.

sowing directly outdoors

You can sow seeds of vegetables, such as carrots and beetroot, and hardy annual flowers directly into your containers outside, rather than starting plants off indoors. And you can also sow tender plants outside from mid-April onwards. Check the seed packet if you're unsure.

Use multipurpose compost or a John Innes seed and cutting compost. If you sow your seeds into too rich a compost the roots may be burnt off due to the high concentration of fertilisers. Either make a drill – a shallow groove – in the surface of the compost and sprinkle in the seed, or simply scatter the seed over the surface – called broadcast sowing.

Then cover the seeds over with compost. Ensure that you water the compost well and don't let it dry out.

Once the seeds germinate and come through the soil, leave them until you can handle the individual seedlings easily. This will normally be when they are between 2–5cm (¾–2in) tall. Then space out or thin the plants – there'll be details of final spacings on the seed packet. Just pull out and discard surplus seedlings, or lift them carefully and replant in another container.

Above: Nicotiana or tobacco flowers. These are just one example of half-hardy annual flowers that can be sown directly into their containers once all danger of frost has passed. **Opposite**: Sow runner beans directly into outside containers from late May to June (or get a head start and sow them indoors in April).

how to plant a pot

It's really simple to transfer plants to their new container. Start by watering the plants well the day before, so the soil surrounding the roots is damp. Set the container in its permanent position and fill up to a third of it with broken crocks or other drainage material. Cover the crocks with a barrier layer (see page 34).

Now fill the container with John Innes No. 3 or multipurpose compost, mixing in one-third by volume horticultural grit or perlite to improve aeration and drainage. Scatter in some slow-release fertiliser granules as you go.

Stand the plant in its current pot inside the container to make a planting hole the size of the root ball. Carefully remove the plant from the pot – you may need to tap it against something hard to loosen the pot. Sit the plant – in this example a dwarf apple tree – in the container and firm the compost round it. Don't overfill: leave about 5cm (2in) between the top of the compost and the rim of the container.

Water really well until water runs out of the drainage holes. Subsequently, allow the compost surface to dry out between watering in the summer, but without letting it become bone-dry.

Above from top: Adding crocks for drainage and a membrane to stop compost blocking the pot's drainage holes; adding slow-release fertiliser granules to the compost as the pot is filled; the apple tree ready to be planted. **Opposite:** A dwarf apple tree standing inside a new container ready to be planted up.

how to prepare a wooden crate

Wood is a natural material that has good insulating properties, keeping roots cool in summer and warm in winter – and it looks great, too. For long life, ensure your crates have been treated with a water-based preservative and have plenty of drainage holes. Raise them on tiles, bricks or pot feet, to prevent rotting at the base.

Drainage and lining

Drill extra drainage holes in the crate before lining it with plastic – an offcut of pondliner is ideal – to stop the sides rotting. Pierce the liner on the base to create drainage holes. Add a layer of broken crocks or similar drainage material, followed by a membrane (see page 34).

Trim the liner and fold it under to create a neat edge before stapling it in position along the top, about 5cm (2in) from the rim of the crate. Fill the crate with multipurpose compost to the depth of the liner, mixing in a handful of slow-release fertiliser granules as you go. Shallow crates are ideal for growing salad leaves; deeper crates can be planted up with almost anything you like.

Above: Onions and potatoes growing in wooden crates. To get enough depth for the potatoes, two old fruit crates were stacked on top of each other, the bottom knocked out of the top crate and the lining continued right down to the depth of two boxes. **Opposite from top**: Assembling the equipment; cutting the liner roughly to size; starting to add a drainage layer and stapling the liner in position; filling with compost; planting up with pak choi.

hanging baskets and window boxes

These two popular methods of container growing bring colour to even the tiniest spaces. Buy conventional boxes or baskets, or make your own hanging baskets using anything from colanders to tin cans – just add a handle.

Lining a traditional hanging basket

Create an all-round display with this clever planting technique. You'll need a traditional 40cm (16in) wire basket and around 35 seedlings. Stand the basket on a 15cm (6in) pot to stop it from moving about. Line the basket with a 3cm (1¼in) layer of soaked sphagnum moss. Place a 3cm (1¼in) layer of multipurpose compost in the bottom of the basket. Place a 10cm (4in) plant saucer on top, to stop water from draining through the basket too quickly. Use a piece of polythene if you do not have a saucer.

Keep 10 seedlings for the top of the basket. Push five seedlings through the first ring of gaps. Place another layer of compost on top of this and then push more plants through the sides until the whole basket is planted, filling with compost as you go along. The compost should come to within 3cm (1¼in) of the top to allow space for watering.

Plant the remaining 10 seedlings over the surface of the basket. Firm the compost, water well and keep in a sheltered position for a week, out of strong sunlight or draughts, before hanging in its final position.

Top: A profusion of begonias, diascias and fuchsias in a sturdy wooden window box.
Above: Fabulous window boxes stuffed to bursting with yellow bidens, dark-leaved dahlias, petunias and geraniums.
Opposite: This colander used as a hanging basket doesn't need lining: once the plant's roots have bound the compost together it won't wash out.

'Trailing fuchsias
are perfect for
hanging baskets
and will bloom all
summer if
deadheaded'

watering containers

You can't rely on the rain to water your pots. Foliage acts like an umbrella and casts the rain off. To water correctly you need to wet the whole volume of compost, not just the top few centimetres. Fill the gap between the surface of the compost and rim of the pot with water – that's why it's important to leave 5cm (2in) between the two – and then let it drain through; repeat several times. Use a watering can or hosepipe (bans permitting), but ensure that the flow rate is not so high that it washes the soil out of the container. I use a spray lance attached to my hosepipe which means I have more control. It also means that I can reach hanging baskets and window boxes easily.

Or try standing containers in a washing-up bowl of water and letting them take up water. Do not leave the plant sitting in water as this can lead to root death. Obviously this method is only useful for smaller pots.

If you have a lot of containers why not consider one of the automatic irrigation systems on the market.

When soilless composts dry out they shrink away from the side of the container and any water then runs straight through the gap. If this happens, immerse the whole container in water and let it soak for 3–4 hours. Adding 3–4 drops of washing-up liquid per gallon of water can help.

Christine's tips

Water plants either first thing in the morning or in the evening. Avoid the middle of the day when temperatures are high and so is the rate of evaporation.

It doesn't have to be a hot sunny day for a container to dry out: dull windy weather can be just as drying. Check pots every day in summer and weekly in winter.

To improve water retention, add water-absorbing gel, available from garden centres, to the compost before planting.

Avoid watering overhead when plants are in flower.

Opposite: Giving a bucket of mint a good soaking.

feeding

Compost contains a limited amount of nutrients and once these are used up, it's time to start feeding your plants. There are three types of feed available.

Liquid feed is a soluble concentrate that you dissolve in water. The nutrients supplied by this method are immediately available to the plant. Liquid feeding needs to be done regularly.

Granular feeds or powders are sprinkled on to the compost and need to be worked into the surface or watered in. They are slower-acting than liquid feeds but tend to be longer-lasting.

Slow-release fertilisers can be granules or cones of resin-coated fertiliser that release the nutrients over a long period of time. Several different formulations are available – some will last 3–6 months, or even a whole season. I use these and then don't have to worry about missing an application of liquid feed.

Different formulations of fertiliser will produce different results. Use a nitrogen-based fertiliser for foliage production, for example, when growing brassicas; a potash one for flowering and fruiting plants; and a high-potash feed when growing both foliage and flowers in the same container. Look on the packet for details.

Above: To get the most from annuals like pansies, you will need to feed regularly all the time they are in flower and growing well.

Christine's tips

Always water a container the day before applying a fertiliser. This reduces the risk of 'burning' the roots and damaging them.

A soil-based compost needs less feeding than a soilless one – follow the instructions on the compost bag.

Only feed when the plants are in active growth, typically from March to September.

Always apply at the manufacturer's recommended dose: overfeeding can burn the roots and damage the plants. Wash off any powders or granules that fall on to the foliage, stems or flowers of any plants.

staking and deadheading

Follow these simple tips to keep your container displays looking their absolute best and productive for as long as possible.

If faded flowers are left on the plant it uses energy to form seeds, which reduces the number of new flowers produced. By deadheading – removing the flowers and the flowering stalk as low as possible on the plant – you will encourage it to produce many more flowers over a long period of time. Plants also look tidier. Use your thumbnail, scissors or a pair of secateurs; whichever method you use, don't crush the flowering stem as this can allow disease to enter the plant.

Do not deadhead vegetables as the flowers go on to produce the crop. Instead harvest beans, peas, courgettes and so on regularly to stimulate the plants to produce more.

Staking

Some plants need a bit of support to look their best. I am a great fan of using twiggy branches pushed into the pot immediately after planting so that the plants can grow over these and hide them completely. Rolls of chicken wire work in a similar way and cane wigwams are great for climbing plants such as sweet peas, morning glory, clematis and runner beans. Push the canes right down into the pot for stability.

Top and above: I do my deadheading on a daily basis. This way, it takes only minutes. **Opposite**: A rustic twiggy wigwam for sweet peas to grow up through.

preventing problems

Sometimes things do go wrong, but growing plants at the right spacing, watering and feeding them correctly will help to reduce the vast majority of problems.

Try to inspect plants every day. This is much easier when plants are growing in pots rather than borders. Often just picking off a diseased or chewed leaf, flower or stem may be enough to stop a problem spreading.

Most pest and disease organisms need shelter and moisture during some part of their life cycle, so make sure there's nowhere they can lurk. Clear away all rubbish. Don't leave old cabbage stalks or other dead or damaged plants in containers to overwinter and remove weeds that may play host to pests and diseases.

Always choose healthy plants from garden centres. Check that they are free from greenfly, for example.

Top: A spinach leaf with typical slug damage. **Above:** The offender apprehended. Never put slugs in your compost heap: they'll thrive and lay eggs, which you'll spread for them next time you mulch your containers or borders. **Opposite:** Net fruit bushes against birds to stop them enjoying the crop before you do.

Christine's tip

Buy or grow resistant varieties. Plant breeders have capitalised on natural plant characteristics such as hairy stems and leaves, waxiness, thick surface layers of leaves, early maturity and vigorous growth, plus other genetic features, to breed new resistant plants. You'll find these features clearly flagged in seed catalogues or plant brochures. Look out for blight-resistant tomatoes and club-root resistant brassicas, and beetroot that are less likely to 'bolt' – flower too early and ruin the crop.

winter care

Plenty of plants are perfectly hardy and can stay in their containers over winter without any extra protection. Borderline-hardy species may need a bit of cosseting. Half-hardy plants, however, can't survive outdoors and should be lifted and potted and placed on a cool windowsill.

Sometimes it's the containers themselves that need protecting, in turn protecting the roots inside. Try wrapping individual pots with bubble wrap. Take the material over the top of the container and tuck over the rim. This helps prevent frost shattering it. Never wrap the actual plant in bubble wrap or polythene as the resulting condensation can cause rotting. Instead surround plants with horticultural fleece or slip a fleece bag over the top.

Group protection

Collecting pots together in a group, packing the gaps between the pots with straw and then placing fleece over the entire group works really well, especially if you group the pots at the base of a south-facing wall. Surrounding the plants with straw held in place with plastic netting is another useful technique.

Always stand pots on pot feet or just use stones, broken slate, slices of wood or old cotton bobbins to raise them off the ground. If a pot freezes, normally it will start to thaw from the top down. If the drainage holes are frozen to the ground, the melt water accumulates in the pot and drowns the plants.

Above and opposite: Use canes and fleece to create a 'tent' to protect plants such as *Geranium palmatum* from frost. Or simply bring a plant's leaves together and wrap them in fleece, holding everything in place with soft twine.

grow your own lunch

Growing vegetables in containers is so easy and rewarding. Eating a delicious salad picked from your patio is a fantastic feeling.

Although any vegetable will grow in a container, the varieties I recommend here are those which have either been bred specifically to be small yet productive or they are those that I know from personal experience do well in pots. And new varieties are coming on to the market all the time.

Colourful lettuces, beetroot and runner beans with their red, white or bi-coloured flowers look just as pretty as all the other ornamental plants you may be growing in containers. So be adventurous in your planting and enjoy the results.

home grown is best

choosing what to grow

Above: Rainbow chard with its amazing stems, and cabbages, fresh from backyard containers. **Opposite**: Mixing the productive with the ornamental on a small patio – pak choi, carrots, broad beans and onions growing in fruit crates against a backdrop of potted auriculas.

What will you grow? That largely depends on what you like eating, but you'll also need to take into account how big your containers are and how sunny the spot is where you've positioned them. Most vegetables do need to grow in full sun and they'll also require frequent watering, so don't site pots too far from a tap or water butt.

The best time to decide is in winter, with your feet up, browsing through the latest seed catalogues. Try not to get carried away – if you've only got a window box or two then stick to a packet of salad leaves or some radishes. If you're not confident about growing from seed (though you should do fine if you follow my advice on pages 36–41), more and more seed suppliers are now selling small plug plants, all ready for you to grow on. Look out for special container vegetable or patio vegetable collections.

The past few years have also seen the introduction of grafted plants for sale. They offer advantages such as increased vigour and heavier crops. They also have greater resistance to pests and diseases and are less susceptible to nutritional disorders. Since they are more vigorous they should be grown in larger containers – in my experience the minimum size is a 30cm (12in) pot. Look out for grafted tomatoes and cucumbers to grow outdoors.

Above. Providing you stake them, and water and feed them well, peas will be happy to grow in an oversized recycled Chinese cooking oil can. **Left**: A larder outside your back door – a pillar of runner beans growing in an old coal hod on one side and a vigorous fig tree on the other.

peas and beans

Runner beans and peas are fabulous climbing plants. If you've got the space, grow full-size varieties (see list) and give them something to scramble up – a wigwam of canes inserted in the container when you plant it up, or fix a piece of trellis or netting against a wall. If space is limited, grow a dwarf variety in a hanging basket or window box.

To get an early start, sow seed in pots on an indoor windowsill (see page 37) and plant them outside once the risk of frost has passed. Or sow direct in your containers in late spring when the compost will have warmed up. Runner beans are prolific – five plants will be plenty for one or two people. Once the plants reach the top of their wigwam or support, nip out the growing point – known as stopping or pinching.

Keep on picking the beans as fast as they are produced. If you leave them on the plant, it will stop flowering and mean no more beans.

Depth is critical

Peas do well in containers that are at least 30cm (12in) deep, so that the compost holds enough water when they are in flower. But ensure there are plenty of drainage holes as peas have a tendency to rot. Stake with twiggy sticks once plants are 10cm (4in) high.

Broad beans need a similar depth container. Space plants 20cm (8in) apart. They look great in a window box, or try growing them in washing-up bowls.

(see page 37)

why not try

BROAD BEANS

'The Sutton' – dwarf variety for exposed areas.

DWARF FRENCH BEANS

'Masterpiece' – early maturing; long, straight, flat pods that can be cooked whole when young.

PEAS

'Meteor' – dwarf pea, growing to about 40cm (16in); small but well-filled pods.

RUNNER BEANS

'Enorma' – tasty long beans.

'Hestia' – dwarf variety stringless beans; attractive bi-coloured red and white flowers.

'Lady Di' AGM – long, slender pods; vigorous.

'Moonlight' – self-pollinating, ensuring a good crop even in poor weather.

'Red Rum' AGM – outstanding self-pollinating variety, cropping heavily.

Below: Stake pea plants (not dwarf varieties); tie them in with soft ties.

courgettes and their relatives

Courgettes are prolific croppers so you really can get a good harvest from container-grown plants. I find that one or two plants are ample – unless you've got a lot of good courgette recipes.

Bush-type courgettes are compact plants suitable for growing in pots – they rarely reach more than 30–45cm (12–18in) tall and 1m (3ft 3in) wide. Don't rule out traditional trailing varieties, though, if you have a balcony or deck – you can train the plants along the railings, or fix trellis or netting to a wall or fence and tie them in with soft ties.

How to grow
Start seeds off indoors in March or April, sow seed direct in containers outside at the end of May/ beginning of June, or buy ready-grown plants. Courgettes need big containers because they need lots of water: the minimum size is a 9 litre (2 gallon) bucket or equivalent. Use a knife to remove the fruit: pulling them by hand leaves a bit of the courgette behind, which tends to go mouldy on the plant and can spread to newly formed courgettes.

All the above sowing and growing advice applies to pumpkins, squashes and outdoor cucumbers.

why not try

COURGETTE

'Buckingham' F1 – compact plant producing lots of thin-skinned yellow fruits with a delicate flavour.

'Midnight' F1 – compact habit with stems and leaves that are spine-free, making harvesting easy. Fruits are dark green and slightly speckled.

'One Ball' F1 – produces round, tennis ball-sized fruit with creamy flesh.

'Patio Star' F1 – I don't think I have ever had so many fruit from one plant as I have with this variety. A good compact plant.

CUCUMBER

'Green Fingers' F1 – productive plant producing mini cucumbers about 9–12cm (3½ – 5in) long. Grow in a 30cm (12in) pot. Tolerant of powdery mildew.

PUMPKIN

'Summer Ball' F1 – treat as a courgette when harvested small or leave to grow on until October as a pumpkin.

'Windsor' F1 – compact variety producing 15cm (6in) fruit.

Opposite: A courgette plant in a substantial bucket with a runner bean tucked in the side and set against a backdrop of euphorbia.

'Rainbow chard looks pretty and is great for salads, or steam the leaves and stalks'

why not try

LETTUCE

'Claremont' AGM – large heads of upright growth.

'Dazzle Red' – 'Little Gem' type, with maroon-red outer leaves and crisp yellow ones inside.

'Little Gem' – small but compact head of green leaves.

'Lollo Rosso' – highly decorative red-leaved variety; adds colour to a salad and is great for edging larger containers.

'Tom Thumb' – a little butterhead type known for its sweet taste.

SALAD MIXES

'Baby Leaf' salad leaves – look out for a mix of spinach, mizuna and red mustard; or for a mix of salad rocket, lettuces 'Lollo Biondi', 'Lollo Rosso', 'Red Salad Bowl', 'Green Salad Bowl' and 'Black Seeded Simpson'.

'Gourmet Mixed' – tasty mix of different shapes and colours.

'Red and Green Salad Bowl Mixed' – both red and green types.

grow your own salad

Salad leaves are quick to grow and productive, making them ideal for beginners. Lettuce can be grown in very little soil, so is perfect for window boxes or shallow trays. As long as you've got around 4cm (1½in) of compost you'll be fine. Simply firm the compost down, sprinkle over the seed, sieve a little more compost on top and water lightly with a fine rose spray.

You should have seedlings pushing through the soil in 7–10 days and you can start picking them in cut-and-come-again fashion (i.e. without cutting the whole plant) in 4–6 weeks. Start sowing outside in late March and make repeat sowings throughout the summer.

The lettuces and chard pictured on this page are growing in colourful buckets that you can buy from garden centres everywhere – just drill some holes for drainage. Lettuces don't need a deep root run so a large proportion of the bucket can be filled with drainage material.

more salad ideas

The speed at which some salad crops grow is amazing. For the first-timer, the experience gained with these can be applied to crops that need more time and skill.

Radishes

Radishes are a really fast crop – you can be harvesting them as little as six weeks after sowing. They're a great way to get children interested in growing. All you need to do is scatter the seed thinly on the surface of the compost in your container and lightly rake it in with a hand fork, then water well.

To avoid tough woody radishes, water frequently, especially in dry weather, to keep them growing rapidly. Harvesting them regularly also stops them turning woody.

Rocket and other leaves

Peppery rocket spices up salads and is easy to grow. Sow seed broadcast in the container, sieve compost on top to cover and water well. Harvest by picking a few leaves from each plant. Do the same with spinach and pak choi. Mustard and cress can be ready to harvest in 7–10 days and is a classic for children to grow in anything from empty egg shells to yogurt pots. Then there's land cress, a tasty alternative to watercress that is much easier to grow – just don't let it dry out.

Top: Wild rocket seedlings almost ready to start picking. **Above:** A selection of oriental salad leaves – you can pick them like this for 'micro salads', or you can transplant and let them grow on to produce bigger plants. **Opposite:** Peppery radishes with just the right amount of crunch without being woody.

sun lovers

Tomatoes, peppers and aubergines are all part of the same family and do best in full sun. You can grow them outside in a sunny sheltered spot in milder areas but you'll need to start them off under cover.

Tomatoes

Have fun growing tomatoes in a kaleidoscope of colours, from yellow to purple-black. There are three types of tomato: cordons, tumbling or bush plants, which cover most growing situations. Try growing tumbling tomato plants in hanging baskets or trailing over the edge of window boxes, or as an edging in containers planted with other veg.

Cordon tomato plants need staking and, to get the best crop, you must pinch out the side shoots when they start to grow. Once about they are about 2cm (¾in) in length, just pinch them out using your finger and thumb. Once the plant has 4–5 groups of flowers, pinch out the growing point at the top of the plant. This will allow the fruits to set and ripen.

Top: Tomato flowers. **Middle**: Trusses of cherry tomatoes at various stages of ripening. **Above**: A fat pleated beefsteak tomato variety. **Opposite**: Tomato leaves showing early signs of magnesium deficiency – a common problem that is easily corrected by spraying the leaves with a solution of 30g (1oz) Epsom salts and a few drops of washing-up liquid in 1 litre (2 pints) of water

 Christine's tip

When growing tomatoes, peppers and aubergines I recommend planting only two plants per growbag. Or grow plants individually in a container at least 30cm (12in) in diameter – this is important to allow enough water to be given and retained by the compost. Use good-quality potting compost. All three crops can be given a liquid feed once the first tiny fruits appear.

why not try

CORDON TOMATOES

'Ailsa Craig' – an old favourite; heavy cropping, producing medium-sized fruits.

'Gardener's Delight' – large cherry-sized, very sweet red fruit. A good variety to start with if you have never grown tomatoes before.

'Golden Pearl' F1 – golden yellow cherry-sized fruit that doesn't seem to crack like some varieties in the late summer.

'Moneymaker' – another good one to try if you are a beginner.

'Olivade' F1 AGM – large, plum-shaped dark red juicy fruit.

'Sungold' F1 – orange, cherry-sized fruit on long trusses. I think this is one of the best-tasting.

'Yellow Perfection' AGM – prolific golden yellow fruits.

TUMBLING AND BUSH TYPES

'Balconi' series – available as either red or yellow fruited; naturally bushy plants.

'Cherry Falls' – good cascading habit; great in window boxes and hanging baskets. Red cherry-sized fruit.

'Little Sun' F1 – compact, bushy plant; yellow cherry-sized fruit.

'Red Robin' – delicious red cherry-fruited variety that grows well in a window box. It is a very compact bush type.

'Tumbler' F1 – vigorous trailing plant, producing up to 4kg (9lb) of cherry-sized red fruit with good flavour; sometimes necessary to support the fruiting branches to prevent them bending.

'Tumbling Tom' series – available either as red, orange or yellow fruited. These plants grow well and need a bit of room so plant in a reasonable-sized basket, 35–45cm (14–18in) in diameter, or in 30cm (12in) pots.

Dwarf and tumbling tomatoes don't need this treatment – just let them get on with it.

Start seed off indoors in March and April. Plant out when risk of frost has passed – this applies to ready-grown plants, too.

Aubergines

As well as the classic dark purple fruits, you can grow gorgeous cream-striped aubergines, long narrow ones and even pure white ones. Follow sowing instructions for tomatoes or buy ready-grown plants and don't put them in their final positions outside until risk of frost has passed.

Aubergines are late cropping, normally producing fruit towards autumn – harvest when the fruits are smooth and glossy and big enough to use. Two plants produce plenty for one person.

Peppers

Sow seed as for tomatoes or buy ready-grown plants. If you've chosen red and yellow varieties, the fruits can take up to six weeks to change colour. They are ready to pick when they are a reasonable size and the skin is glossy. Keep picking to keep the plant producing – leaving peppers on the plant reduces the harvest. The same advice applies to chilli peppers and you should start picking the fruits while they are still immature, to extend the growing season.

Top and above: Aubergines come in all shapes. The flowers are pretty but watch out for the spines. **Opposite**: Yellow chilli peppers and red sweet peppers against a sheltered wall.

mix it up

There's a lot to be said for intensive planting. The close proximity of the plants creates a warm sheltered microclimate, as well as making a fabulous display. The densely planted corner in the photo opposite has tall sweetcorn and beans growing in lined wicker containers underplanted with courgettes and nasturtiums, with some kale in the background.

Mutual benefits

Sweetcorn plants benefit from being grown in a group as they rely on the wind to pollinate the flowers and to form the corn cobs. The leaves of the courgette will shade all the plants' roots and help prevent evaporation.

Nasturtium flowers make a nice faintly spicy addition to salads – though watch out for blackfly. In fact some gardeners grow nasturtiums as a 'sacrificial' crop to lure these pests away from more precious plants. Start sweetcorn, beans and courgettes off indoors in individual pots and plant them out when all risk of frost has passed. Sow nasturtiums directly into the container, pressing seeds lightly into the gaps between the plants.

Kale can be sown direct, too, from May to July – it's a surprisingly ornamental plant that will keep going all through the winter. It's good to look at and good to eat – healthy *and* delicious.

why not try

KALE

'Dwarf Green Curled' – ideal for containers.

'Black Tuscany' – stunning black leaves.

'Cavolo Nero' – rich green narrow leaves.

SWEETCORN

'Sweetie Pie' F1 – good variety for growing in a 35cm (14in) diameter pot; very sweet and early maturing. Put 6 plants per pot.

'Incredible' F1 – very sweet, fast-growing plant producing long cobs with good tolerance to common rust; ideal in wet summers.

BEANS – see page 67.

COURGETTES – see page 69.

root vegetables

Root crops do well in containers as the light structure of the potting compost helps them to form uniform roots – important for carrots and beetroot. Don't attempt to transplant thinnings when sowing direct as they won't do well – try adding to salads instead.

Beetroot

Striking red stems and leaf veins make beetroot plants attractive enough to grow in among flowers. In the garden opposite they're growing in a pot set in the top of an old chimney. Once they've been harvested the pot can be whisked away and another one set in its place – that's the beauty of container gardening. Sow seed directly into outdoor containers from March to July. The seeds are large: they're capsules containing several seeds, so you may need to thin out seedlings. Space seeds 10cm (4in) apart and push them down into the compost to around 2cm (¾in) deep.

Carrots

Carrots have ferny foliage that looks great with ornamental plants. For a mixed container, start carrots off in small pots, sowing two to three seeds in each. Transplanting all three seedlings to their final container will produce small carrots – or thin to the strongest and grow that one on. When growing only carrots in the container, sow directly, scattering seeds thinly, then sieving 2cm (¾in) compost on top. Thin out to 5cm (2in).

why not try

BEETROOT

'Pablo' F1 AGM – uniform round beets that can stay in the ground for a long time.

'Wodan' F1 AGM – bright red beets that can be harvested small or left to grow without getting woody; use young leaves like spinach.

CARROTS

'Early Market' – good for sowing right through the spring and summer. Stump-rooted.

'Rondo' – tasty globe-shaped carrot.

Below: For shallow containers like this wooden veg box, choose a stump-rooted variety of carrot.

Potatoes

Growing potatoes in a container will probably only produce enough for one meal – but what a meal. Nothing beats freshly dug new potatoes with butter and a sprig of mint. I recommend growing early varieties that will crop in July or August. Maincrop potatoes aren't ready until later in the year and so they'll occupy containers for a long time and won't look that attractive later in the season.

Use a purpose-made potato bag to grow potatoes or a large container at least 30cm (12in) deep. Add the usual drainage layer (see page 35) then add 10–15cm (4–6in) of multipurpose compost. Place three sprouted seed potatoes on top and cover with 10cm (4in) of compost.

Once the plants are growing and have produced 15cm (6in) of leaf growth, fill the container with another 10cm (4in) of compost. This is the equivalent of earthing up – done when growing potatoes in the ground – and will partly bury the plant. Do not worry about this as it encourages tuber formation on these buried stems.

When the leaves have produced another 15cm (6in) of growth, top up with another 10cm (4in) of compost; keep repeating this until the surface of the compost is within 5cm (2in) of the top. Harvesting can be done in two stages: pushing your hand down on to the compost to lift potatoes from the upper part of the container; to reach those lower down, tip out the container once you have harvested those from the top. If you've used a potato bag, open the flap and pull them out.

why not try

POTATOES

'Charlotte' AGM – salad type 2nd early with creamy yellow flesh. Plant mid–late April, harvest August.

'Foremost' 1st early – white-fleshed tubers with excellent taste. Plant late March/early April, harvest July.

'Rocket' 1st early – waxy egg-sized potatoes with pure white flesh. Plant late March/early April, harvest July.

'Vivaldi' 2nd early – oval yellow-skinned potatoes with pale yellow flesh. Plant mid–late April, harvest August.

Christine's tips

Before you plant seed potatoes they must be left to form shoots – a process known as chitting. I stand the potatoes on end, with 'eyes' at the top, in old egg boxes and leave them in a light place for about six weeks. When the shoots are 2.5cm (1in) long, they're ready to plant.

Potatoes are heavy feeders so feed with a high phosphorus liquid fertiliser following the manufacturer's instructions.

If frost is forecast cover the foliage with horticultural fleece.

Opposite: Harvesting the first of the early summer potatoes – you can get them from pot to plate in less than 30 minutes.

lunch in a barrel

Make yourself a mini market garden in a barrel and enjoy tender baby carrots, mini beetroots and fresh-picked peas straight from the pod. There's plenty of room for all in a barrel as the peas like to scramble upwards, leaving space at their feet. (For information on growing beets and carrots, see page 83.) Peas can be sown directly into containers from mid-March to July. Push old twiggy prunings into the compost to make a scaffold for them to climb or tie canes into a wigwam. Pick regularly to encourage more flowering. Dwarf peas are great in hanging baskets or window boxes.

Heaven on a plate

The most extraordinary thing about home-grown produce is that you really don't need very much to make a meal. When you have grown it yourself, you savour every last tiny leaf!

For a summer salad take a few baby beets and carrots, leaving the root tail on each, and lightly boil or steam. Rinse some young beet leaves and arrange on your favourite plate. Sprinkle sweet raw peas on top. Add the warm beets and carrots, a few lightly boiled eggs cut in half, keeping the yolks semi-soft. Finish with an oil, vinegar and honey dressing.

Opposite and below: Peas need lots of water when they come into flower so grow them in a big container like a barrel, at least 30cm (12in) deep. Train the peas upwards and there'll be plenty of room at their feet for the carrots and beetroots.

brassicas and greens

The spacing at which you grow plants can have a direct effect on the size of the mature plant, particularly in the case of cabbages. But rather than using trial and error to manipulate your crop, sow or buy patio or container brassicas specially developed by plant breeders.

Be firm
A beautiful dense cabbage head in a classic terracotta pot is just as attractive as the non-edible ornamental sort. To get the best results, start seedlings off outside then transplant to their final container. Plant them deeply so that their lower leaves are at soil level and firm the compost round them really well – this is crucial to success with cabbages. The container should be at least 30cm (12in) deep.

Other brassicas to try
Calabrese or green sprouting broccoli is underrated in my opinion. It is fast-growing, producing heads 80–90 days after sowing direct in a container. Sow seed in groups of three, 30cm (12in) apart, and thin to the strongest seedling once 8cm (3in) tall. Keep picking to stimulate more growth. 'Green Magic' F1 is early maturing, from June to August, and produces tightly packed heads. Kale is a hardy brassica that you can go on picking right through winter and it looks great in containers (see also page 81).

Above: Brassica seedlings more than ready to transplant. **Opposite**: Purple kale is fabulously ornamental and so delicious. Harvest young leaves and shoots but don't strip the plant, so that it will go on to produce more leaves.

growing
herbs in
containers

Herbs are not only great for everyday use in the kitchen but make fantastic ornamental subjects when grown in containers. And by using separate containers, you can grow herbs that need free-draining soil alongside those that prefer wetter conditions. Herbs are available in all sorts of sizes, shapes, colours and textures, from annuals to perennials.

Their fragrant leaves or flowers, and sometimes both, can be enjoyed by all members of the family. I use them in cooking, for snipping over salads, for making hot drinks, adding fragrance to the house, and in the bath. I always feel that their aroma brings my garden indoors for me.

herbs

parsley, sage, rosemary and thyme...

why not try

Flat-leaf parsley *Petroselinum crispum* var. *neapolitanum* – low-growing annual.

Lemon thyme *Thymus citriodorus* – evergreen perennial 15cm (6in) tall. Lemon-scented leaves.

Marjoram *Origanum vulgare* – 45cm (18in) perennial with clusters of small purple flowers.

Rosemary *Rosmarinus officinalis* – evergreen perennial up to 1m (3ft 3in) tall.

Sage *Salvia officinalis* – perennial growing to 60cm (24in). Aromatic oval, grey-green leaves.

I enjoy growing herbs in a window box so I can see them from indoors as well as outside. They look ornamental and are very handy for picking, so plant your window box with herbs that you use frequently.

These are the stalwarts of a kitchen garden. One of the easiest-to-grow herbs is thyme. It comes in many different forms: creeping thyme does as it says and hugs the ground and there are several variegated thymes that garden designers love for their delicate grey-green foliage; but for fragrance, flavour and hardiness you can't beat common thyme or *Thymus vulgaris*. The flowers attract bees and butterflies, but as with all herbs it's best not to let it flower if you want full-strength culinary flavour.

At the end of the season thyme often needs to be cut back, so don't waste it. Hang bunches upside down in a warm dry place. After a couple of weeks strip the leaves off the stems and transfer to an airtight jar.

Below: Silver-leaved and dark green varieties of thyme make a subtle contrast.
Opposite: Thyme in full flower in an elaborate miniature urn – keep it on the patio table and sprinkle the leaves over new potatoes, bacon and tomatoes if you're eating al fresco.

 Christine's tip

Always pick herbs in the early morning or in the evening, when the plants will be turgid (full of water) and at their most flavoursome.

summer herbs

why not try

Basil *Ocimum basilicum* – annual growing to 45cm (18in). A classic for use with tomato dishes and for making pesto.

Basil 'Aristotle' – a compact plant with tiny leaves; great for outdoor growing.

Basil 'Sweet Genovese' – large-leaved basil, easy to grow. Remove flowers to increase leaf production.

Chives *Allium schoenoprasum* – perennial growing to 30cm (12in). Purple globe flowers. Leaves and flowers have a mild onion flavour.

Dill *Anethum graveolens* – annual growing up to 1.5m (5ft) and producing small yellowish green flowers through the summer. Both leaves and seeds have many culinary uses.

Fennel *Foeniculum vulgare* – perennial up to 2m (6½ft) tall, with feathery green foliage and yellow flowers in summer. Both the foliage and seeds may be used in cooking. A lovely bronze form *F. v.* 'Purpureum' is available, which is not only a lovely herb but a great ornamental plant as well. Use with pork, fish and salads.

French tarragon *Artemisia dracunculus* – perennial up to 90cm (36in) tall. Long narrow leaves with an anise flavour. Protect from rain in winter.

Winter tarragon *Tagetes lucida* – tender perennial growing up to 80cm (32in) with oval mid-green leaves. I think this has more of a taste of aniseed than French tarragon.

Opposite: A collection of basils in warm Mediterranean terracotta pots.

Basil, tarragon, dill, fennel, coriander, chervil and chives are all herbs with fleshy stems and softer leaves so they require a little more attention. You can grow them from seed if you start them off indoors. Only put them outside when you are certain the frosts are over. The extra care will pay off when you add torn basil leaves to your home-grown tomato salad or your own pesto sauce.

Summer herbs and pasta

Gently sauté chopped parsley, basil and chives, freshly picked and halved cherry tomatoes, fresh chilli (optional) and garlic in olive oil; toss your favourite cooked pasta into the fragrant herby mixture and serve with grated Parmesan cheese.

Herb butter

Finely chop tarragon, fennel, chives or chervil and add to softened butter with some sea salt and a squeeze of lemon juice. Blend with a fork and then spread on to clingfilm and roll into a sausage. Twist the ends tightly and keep in the fridge, slicing off discs when required. Great for baking or grilling fish.

versatile mint

Mint is a highly invasive grower and will spread into borders or beds, quickly swamping other plants, so the best way of preventing this is to grow it in a container. This can be a traditional plant pot but I think mint looks great when grown in a hanging basket, either on its own or with other mint varieties. Set your container or hanging basket in full sun or light/dappled shade. If you do plant different varieties close together, be aware they can hybridise and produce intermediate forms. You might have to start again with new plants after a couple of years.

Cooking with mint

You can never, ever have too much mint – one minute you are cursing it for spreading and taking over your carefully planted window box and the next minute you are searching for more to make some mint sauce. Peas and new potatoes are so much tastier when cooked with mint, and fresh mint tea is a delight on a hot afternoon – just pick a handful, stuff into the teapot and pour on boiling water – far better than any of those dull mint teabags.

Sweet or savoury

Mint is one of the few herbs that works equally well in sweet or savoury dishes. Try slicing strawberries in half, sprinkling with caster sugar and then adding torn mint leaves. Delicious!

why not try

Corsican mint *Mentha requienii* – a tiny plant just 2cm (¾in) tall with peppermint-scented leaves making flat, mat-like growth.

Creeping pennyroyal *Mentha pulegium* – low-growing mint only 5cm (2in) tall. Strongly peppermint-scented small leaves. Rarely flowers.

Hart's pennyroyal *Mentha cervina* – perennial producing attractive clusters of mauve flowers in late summer. Narrow mid-green peppermint-scented leaves. Do not allow plants to dry out. Grows to 20cm (8in).

Peppermint *Mentha x piperita* – vigorous creeping perennial growing to about 45cm (18in) tall, producing purple/pink flowers from summer to autumn. Very dark brown oval leaves; strongly peppermint scented.

Spearmint *Mentha spicata* – perennial up to 60cm (24in) tall with mid-green oval leaves. Small purple flowers in summer.

Upright pennyroyal *Mentha pulegium* 'Upright' – perennial semi-evergreen mint 15cm (6in) tall with clusters of mauve flowers in spring.

lavender

I lead garden tours to France in the summer and always really enjoy visiting the lavender fields for their fragrance. At home I grow my lavenders in large metal buckets: their colour complements the lavender and also the handles make moving them about really easy. On the patio on a warm summer's day I am transported back to France and those lovely fields.

My perception is that French lavender is an ornamental plant – it's got those pretty little 'bunny ears' flowers and English lavender is the type to grow for flavouring and cooking.

Keeping lavender in good shape

To stop lavender going woody and straggly, cut off the flowers immediately they've finished – this encourages basal growth and new leaves, which is what you need if you want to grow lavender as a herb crop. Most people make the mistake of leaving the flowers on far too long, so that the plant puts all its energy into producing seed – perfect for making lavender bags or pot pourri but the plant then goes woody and, when you do prune it, it pops its clogs.

Above: English lavenders are best for culinary use – this plant is due for pruning shortly, once more flowers have faded.
Opposite: Two different shades of French lavender (*Lavandula stoechas*) showing their typical bunny-eared flowers.

Eau de Cologne mint *Mentha* x *piperita* f. *citrata* –
perennial with amazing scented leaves.

Lavender 'Hidcote' – bushy dwarf plant; grows to
50cm (20in) with deep purple flowers.

Lemon balm *Melissa officinalis* – I love this plant
for its lemon-scented leaves. It grows up to 75cm
(30in). Useful in cooking or in the bath.

Lemon verbena *Aloysia triphylla* – needs winter
protection. Gorgeous lemon-scented leaves.

Prostrate rosemary *Rosmarinus officinalis*
Prostratus Group – low-growing perennial.

Scented pelargoniums *Pelargonium* Fragrans
Group – scented leaves in rose, lemon, orange and
mint, to name a few.

Below: Lemon balm, rosemary, scented
pelargonium and lavender tied up in
muslin for a blissfully relaxing bath.

bathtime herbs

An old butler's sink with its plughole for built-in drainage makes an unusual feature for growing herbs to scent a bath. Use any combination of herbs but my favourites are lemon balm, rosemary, lemon verbena, lavender (*Lavandula angustifolia* 'Hidcote' has a lovely classic fragrance), mint and scented geranium.

Making a bath bag

I have found the best method of using the herbs for this purpose is to get a square piece of muslin or very fine gauze, place several stems of herbs in the middle, tie it all up in a bundle and then hang it under the hot tap so that the water runs through it. I only use this bundle once, while a lot of other people say they use it several times. I have so much material to hand I like it to be fresh each time.

 Christine's tip

You can also dry the herbs and sew into a muslin bag to hang in
your wardrobe or place in clothes drawers.

the patio
orchard

You can grow fruit in the smallest and most unpromising of spaces. Over the years I have enjoyed harvesting my own apples from small trees specially bred for container growing. Add growbags planted with strawberries, tall tubs of raspberries and you've got the makings of a mini orchard. And redcurrant bushes will even put up with a bit of shade. So there really is something to grow for everyone and every situation.

Nothing that you buy from the supermarket will beat the taste of a handful of home-grown strawberries. Your main competitors for berry crops will be the birds – be vigilant, particularly when fruit starts to ripen.

pick your very own

why not try

STRAWBERRIES

EARLY-SUMMER VARIETIES (mid-June to early July)

'Christine' – good levels of natural sweetness.

'Honeoye' AGM – popular garden variety.

MID-SUMMER VARIETIES (late June to mid-July)

'Cambridge Late Pine' – possibly the best-tasting variety ever produced.

'Hapil' AGM – heavy cropper.

LATE-SUMMER VARIETIES (throughout July)

'Fenella' – good sweet flavour.

'Florence' – heavy cropper.

PERPETUAL FRUITING VARIETIES (mid-August to mid-October; may also crop in early summer)

'Albion' – large aromatic fruit.

'Flamenco' – heavy cropper.

Christine's tips

Liquid feeding weekly with a tomato fertiliser will improve performance, but allow the plants to establish for four weeks before feeding.

Remove any runners the plants produce after fruiting. In November remove all the old leaves.

summer berries

Juicy strawberries and raspberries are a sure sign that summer is here, and how much nicer if you can pick your very own just outside the back door. Experiment with different varieties to find your favourites.

Strawberries
Nowadays you can plant up a pot of strawberries and be eating the sweetest, juiciest fruit in just two months. It's all down to new varieties and production methods. Buy cold-stored runners – available from mail order suppliers from late March/April to late July – plant outdoors between May and July, and the plants will crop in about 60 days.

Keep watering
Strawberries can be grown very successfully in window boxes, hanging baskets, flower pouches, tower pots, strawberry pots, and all sorts of containers. All you have to do is watch that the compost doesn't dry out – this can cause the flowers to drop off or the fruit to stop growing.

A large growbag, for example, will have space for 10 plants and give you several punnets of fruit. If you want strawberries all summer, choose varieties that fruit at different times: plan it right and you'll have berries for breakfast from June to October.

Raspberries

Plant up a tub of delicious raspberries close to the kitchen door so you can nip out and pick the fruit as it ripens. Small children love picking raspberries: the fruit grows at just the right height, but warn them about spiny stems – or grow spine-free varieties.

Mail order bare-root canes are delivered between December and March ready for planting. You'll need a large container, at least 60cm (24in) deep, and a soil-based compost such as John Innes No. 3. Plant canes to the same depth as they were growing – look for the change in colour on the stem: the area that was below ground will be darker. Keep the top of the dark section level with the compost's surface.

Water well to settle the compost around the roots and keep the pots well watered all summer. Feed regularly with a high-potash fertiliser according to the manufacturer's recommendations.

Pruning

Autumn-fruiting varieties bear fruit on the current season's new growth. They should not need any supports. Each February just cut the canes down to soil level to encourage new cane growth. Prune away the old canes of summer-fruiting varieties in autumn. The raspberries pictured here were trained spirally round their wigwam supports by tying in the long soft growth. This not only looks neater but boosts berry production, too.

Blackberries, tayberries and other cane fruits can also be grown in pots but the main problem is their height – 2.5m (8ft) canes can seriously destabilise a container.

why not try

RASPBERRIES

SUMMER-FRUITING VARIETIES

'Glen Moy' – heavy cropping, compact. Container must have good drainage. Spine free, so great for children to grow.

'Glen Prosen' – canes are spine free and easy to control.

'Malling Jewel' – consistent moderate crops with good flavour.

AUTUMN-FRUITING VARIETIES

'Autumn Bliss' AGM – always does well, even in a bad season.

'Autumn Treasure' – pest and disease resistance; a good choice for the organic gardener.

'Joan' – outstanding new variety with spine-free canes.

'Polka' – exceptionally large succulent fruit with an intense flavour.

Above: Trained fruit takes up much less space on a patio or balcony. Here whitecurrant 'White Grape' has been trained into a two-dimensional fan, ideal for standing against a wall or fence.
Left: A 'Red Lake' redcurrant bush has been trained into an espalier shape, with branches tied into canes set parallel with the ground. Both techniques are also suitable for jostaberries or Oregon thornless blackberries.

See also pages 116–17 for more bushes trained to grow flat against a wall or fence. Buy bushes ready-trained from a specialist nursery and ask for advice on pruning and further training.

fruity shrubs

Grow a rainbow of coloured fruits on these perennial shrubs which will keep on fruiting for years if you feed, water and prune them correctly. Train into formal shapes to make them even more decorative.

Red, white and blackcurrants

Translucent redcurrants add a jewel garnish to fruit salads and tarts yet are rarely on sale except in top-notch supermarkets or farmers' markets. Whitecurrants are even scarcer. Luckily, along with blackcurrants, they are very easy to grow in containers.

Choose a container at least 40cm (16in) deep and fill it with multipurpose compost or John Innes No. 3, mixing in some slow-release fertiliser at the manufacturer's recommended rate. Don't forget to leave a 5cm (2in) gap between compost and rim so that you can give the pots a real good soaking. In summer water the pots well, so that you see the water draining out of the bottom of the container. In hot weather this may be necessary every couple of days.

Harvesting

Harvest the entire string of currants when they have turned a good colour – red, white or black. They will keep for about a week in the fridge or you can freeze them. Or try dipping them in egg white then caster sugar for an elegant garnish for desserts.

why not try

REDCURRANTS

'Rovada' – late-ripening variety producing long trusses in August.

WHITECURRANTS

'White Versailles' – sweet, pale yellow fruits ready to harvest in July.

BLACKCURRANTS

'Ben Lomond' – upright bush with shiny jet-black berries that are sweet-tart and excellent for jams. Fruit ripens towards the end of July.

Pruning tips

Both currants and gooseberries produce fruit on branches that are at least two years old. Follow this pruning regime to boost your berry crop:

In the first year allow the plant to establish.

In year two between November and March select five or six healthy stems evenly spaced around the bush and prune all the others off at the base. The branches that have been left will be two years old and should bear fruit. New branches will appear from the base of the plant.

In year three remove two of the oldest branches and select five or six of the branches produced this year. Prune off any other branches produced this year.

From year four prune out a third of all the old branches and remove anything diseased, damaged, misplaced or dead.

Gooseberries

Gooseberries come in a range of colours from yellowy to olive green and pinky red. Their flavours vary widely, too, from sweet-tart to aromatic apricot. Dessert gooseberries can be eaten straight from the bush; culinary ones make great crumbles, fools and jams and preserves.

Plant gooseberries using the same instructions for currants (see page 113) and follow the same pruning regime to keep your bushes productive. Growing gooseberries as fans (see opposite) is not only decorative, it keeps the air circulating round the leaves and fruit and reduces the chances of the bush developing mildew. You also tend to get larger fruits. Gooseberries are ready to pick when they ripen to the appropriate colour and are slightly soft. They will last for about 10 days in the fridge or may be frozen.

Blueberries

Expensive to buy in supermarkets yet easy to grow in containers, the bushes do best in a sheltered site. Most importantly, they need moisture-retentive acidic compost – or ericaceous compost – and are fine in sun or part shade.

Select a container a couple of sizes up from the size of pot the plant was supplied in. If you bought it in a 25cm (10in) pot, plant it into a container no smaller than 27cm (10¾in). Do not use grit for drainage as it may contain lime and so damage the plants. I have found polystyrene beads to be best. In hard-water areas, collect rainwater in a butt to water them.

why not try

GOOSEBERRIES

'Duke' AGM – one of the heaviest and most reliable of croppers, ripening early July. Protect flowers from the frost by covering the plants with fleece. Lovely autumn leaf colour makes this a highly ornamental plant as well as productive.

'Spartan' AGM – one of the best-flavoured varieties. Large fruit with a sweet tangy flavour from early July. Leaves turn a beautiful shade of orange and yellow in the autumn.

BLUEBERRIES

'Sunshine Blue' – attractive bright pink flowers that fade to white; heavy crops of medium-sized berries in July. Semi-evergreen.

Look out for duo-minarettes where two varieties are
grown on one stem.

COOKING APPLES

'Bountiful' – dual dessert and culinary apple.

'Howgate Wonder' – good for northerly areas.

EATING APPLES

'Discovery' – good flavoured crisp apple.

'Kidd's Orange Red' – a late dessert apple with
sweet aromatic flesh.

'Pixie' – crisp, juicy and aromatic.

CHERRIES

'Lapins' – round heart-shaped fruit which is firm,
sweet and juicy. Ripens July.

NECTARINES

'Early Rivers' – large fruit with a pale straw-
coloured skin with a pink flush. Self-fertile.

PEACHES

'Peregrine' – one of the best-flavoured peaches
around with very juicy sweet flesh and bearing
heavy crops. Self-fertile. Early August.

PEARS

'Beth' – a medium-sized pear with sweet flavour.

DESSERT PLUMS

'Blue Tit' – very juicy dessert plums that cook well.
Very hardy. Ripens mid-August.

Opposite, clockwise from left:
A lemon tree; Red Windsor apple;
Victoria plums; lemon; and
calamondin (miniature orange).
You can grow just about any tree in
a pot if it's on a dwarf rootstock.
The best rootstocks for container
growing are – apple: M9, M26; pear:
'Quince C'; plum, damson, peach,
nectarine: 'Pixy' or 'St Julien A';
apricot: 'St Julien A' or 'Torinel'.

tree fruits

Most fruit trees can be grown in a container: apples,
pears, cherries, plums, damsons, peaches, nectarines
and apricots. The key is to choose varieties grown
on the right root system or rootstock. The rootstock
controls the plant's vigour. Look for the information
on the label when buying your tree.

Trees can be planted into containers at any time of
the year, but in practice I have found planting in
March and April works best, as the trees soon root
into the compost and establish quickly. The container
needs to be at least 45–50cm (18–20in) in diameter.
Follow the instructions on pages 42–3.

Citrus trees do well in pots but must be kept under
cover in winter: make sure you have space indoors.

To prevent tree roots becoming pot bound, repot
every alternate year, after leaf fall. Once in the final
pot, the plants can be root-pruned every other year
and 30 per cent of the old compost renewed.

 Christine's tip

Pollination is vital for the vast majority of fruiting trees, otherwise
you won't get any fruit. Providing you grow at least two trees from
the same pollination group (or a close one – ask for advice when
you buy your young trees), all should be well. Or choose self-fertile
varieties, though you'll always get a better crop with two self-fertile
trees rather than one.

growing flowers
in containers

Pots of flowers can transform the most unpromising outdoor space into somewhere inviting to sit and linger. Without any flowers growing in containers, my patio would look pretty ugly. It is where I tend to concentrate highly fragrant plants so that when I go out of my kitchen door I'm engulfed with wonderful scents. You can also stage-manage your display, bringing pots just about to burst into bloom to the fore and moving those just past their peak to the back – provided the pots aren't too heavy, of course. Choose the right plants and you can even grow enough flowers for cutting; that way you'll bring the garden right into your home.

the power of flowers

all about bulbs

Bulbs are perfect candidates for container growing. With a little planning you can have bulbs in bloom all the year round, starting with the earliest snowdrops, crocus and scillas, and going on to daffodils and all the spring-flowering bulbs, then summer lilies and dahlias, autumn-flowering crocus and the winter flowering cyclamen. Add them in a layer in window boxes below the rest of the plants for a flower-packed display that makes maximum use of space. Or plant pots of single varieties, matching the size of the plant to the pot for scale and stability. As a general rule of thumb, plant bulbs at twice the depth of their size, though there are some exceptions – check pack label for instructions. Cyclamen should be planted with the tubers just in the surface of the compost. Good drainage is very important, to prevent them rotting.

After flowering

Once they've flowered, let the bulbs die down fully in situ to allow them to build up their reserves for the following season. Once their leaves have fully withered, you can pull them off and remove bulbs from the container. Brush off any soil and store them in paper bags, in a cool dry place, ready for planting next year. Whenever possible, the vast majority of bulbs that have been in containers are best planted out in the open garden, where they have greater access to water and nutrients, rather than back into a container. Plant spring-flowering bulbs in autumn, summer bulbs in late spring/early summer and autumn bulbs by late summer.

Top: Dwarf daffodils mixed with crocus. Dwarf daffodils grow to around 15cm (6in), perfect for small pots or window boxes. Here they are mixed with crocus 'Pickwick', which is also growing in the pot in the foreground. **Above**: Chionodoxa has starry blue flowers in spring and grows to just 10–20cm (4–8in). **Opposite**: White daffodils in sturdy mosaic pots against a backdrop of lime-green euphorbia.

Iris danfordiae – miniature iris, 5–10cm (2–4in) with scented yellow flowers.

IRIS RETICULATA VARIETIES

'George'– large maroon/plum-coloured flowers with yellow markings.

'Harmony' – deep velvety-blue with clear white and yellow tips. Flowering at 15cm (6in) tall.

'Joyce' – large sky-blue flowers with ivory tips. Leaves grow to 30cm (12in) after flowering.

IRIS HISTRIOIDES VARIETIES

'Angel's Tears' – delicate shades of blue and white with golden markings.

'Katharine Hodgkin' – slate-blue veining over the flowers – a real show-stopper. An easy and reliable bulb.

SNOWDROP (GALANTHUS) VARIETIES

'Flore Pleno' – honey-scented double flowers and grey-green leaves, 10–15cm (4–6in).

'S. Arnott' – strongly scented white flowers with a green edge on inner petals, 20cm (8in).

early arrivals

February can be a barren time for container gardeners but if you plan ahead and plant the very early flowering bulbs in October and November you will be rewarded with some lovely early arrivals in February or even late January if you are really lucky

Snowdrops are an obvious choice and there are many, many different types. It's easy to see why some people become hooked: galanthophiles, as they're known, can pay hundreds of pounds for rare bulbs. Grape hyacinths and miniature irises make for a welcoming array if you have a front step or porch and will cheer up a grey winter's day.

Getting them started

Plant in compost that has good drainage. Remember to water but don't overdo it – bulbs don't like sitting in waterlogged soil – and plant the bulbs to a depth that is twice that of the bulb.

You can mix small varieties up with other bulbs but, as they flower at different times, some of the shorter varieties can get hidden by the foliage of the later bloomers, so go for several bulbs of the same variety in each pot for maximum impact. Or stagger the planting depths in your container, starting with a layer of later-flowering bulbs such as dwarf tulips, covering them with compost and then adding layers of early-flowering bulbs on top.

colour and drama

If you have a small balcony in the city or a corner of a paved patio that needs brightening up, think about going for bold coloured pots to complement or contrast bright flowers.

Terracotta goes with everything but if you have a couple of the popular imported deep blue or turquoise-green glazed pots, then think about planting deep blue lobelia in them for real designer impact. Who says blue and green should not be seen?

French marigolds are often seen in formal park-plantings in large quantities. But why not take a couple of these easy-to-grow and abundant flowering gems and place them in a black or even an orange planter. Now you get the idea, the possibilities are endless. Red impatiens in a shiny red pot look terrific; so do black grasses in a matt black pot – or try vice versa to make dramatic contrasts. Be bold and be brave. Your balcony will become a fashion statement!

Above: Stunning azure lobelia flowers cascade from a glazed pot. **Opposite**: Zingy orange French marigolds are a perfect match for a bright orange cup and saucer.

Christine's tip

Smaller pots dry out very quickly, so don't forget to place saucers of water underneath if you go away for a few days. The specially made cup opposite has a hole in the bottom for drainage – and a saucer to hold the water. It's amazing what you can find in garden centres and gift shops these days.

sweet peas and climbers

why not try

SWEET PEAS

'Bouquet Mixed' – large blooms on sturdy stems. One of the best for cutting.

'Fragrantissima' – selection of colours producing good-quality blooms and intense fragrance. Excellent cut flower.

'Kings Chelsea Scented Collection' – nine specially selected varieties for the best sweet-pea fragrance.

DWARF SWEET PEAS

'Cupid Mixed' – the best cupid dwarf sweet peas, in plain and picotee colours.

'Patio Mixed' – dwarf habit and masses of flowers, each stem producing up to four blooms.

'Sugar 'n' Spice Mixed' – 18cm (7in) trailing plant; compact in habit and just as sweetly scented as its taller cousins.

Sweet peas are one of the easiest climbers to grow. Buy plants from a garden centre or grow your own from seed. When the seedlings are about 10–15cm (4–6in) tall, remove 2cm (¾in) from the growing point, using a pair of scissors or your thumbnail. This is known as pinching out and will encourage the plants to produce more than one shoot.

Planting up your container

Do this in late March once you've hardened the seedlings off. Water the plants the day before. Place a 45cm (18in) container in its final position and fill, following the instructions on pages 34–5. Place six bamboo canes, rustic hazel poles or long twiggy prunings equidistantly inside the rim of the container, then bring them together at the top and tie with string to form a wigwam. Plant two seedlings around the base of each cane. Water well.

As the plants start to grow up the poles, tie them in with some soft string. Ensure that they do not dry out and start liquid feeding in June. Once they start to flower, keep cutting the flowers. If you leave them on the plant to form seedpods this reduces flowering. It also means sweet-scented posies for the house.

Other annual climbers to try include *Ipomoea tricolor* 'Heavenly Blue' (morning glory), *Mina lobata* (syn. *Ipomoea lobata*) and *Cobaea scandens* (cup and saucer vine).

annual visitors

For me, summer is about experiencing the full
impact of colour that comes from annual bedding
plants. From window boxes full of fabulous petunias
in rainbow shades, to pots packed with pansies and
unusual containers such as the tin bath opposite
– they all say: here comes summer and colour.
The pink pelargoniums in the tin bath are strictly
speaking half-hardy perennials but we tend to treat
them as annuals. If you have space, try overwintering
yours in a frost-free place: cut the plants down and
keep them barely watered.

Below: Easy-to-grow pansies come in an
astounding range of colours and flower
shapes, from single to double, and can
be raised from seed or bought cheaply.
Deadhead regularly to keep them flowering.

'Fabulous annual petunias will flower all summer long if you deadhead them regularly'

portable planting

This is the ultimate way to get a splash of colour just where you want it. What could be easier to move than a wicker basket full of antirrhinums or a bright plastic shopper with dazzling bedding plants? And for sheer mobility – not to mention eye-catching quirkiness – think outside the box and plant anything that's not in use and gathering dust, just like this doll's pram (below left).

To plant the baskets, simply line with plastic, piercing drainage holes in the base of the liner, then follow the instructions on pages 44–5, tucking the edges of the liner neatly below the rim of the basket so that they don't show. There are many varieties of antirrhinums: here I've used tall ones but if you wanted to show off the handle more, use dwarf varieties instead.

The doll's pram doesn't need to be filled with compost to such a depth for small plants; you could probably fill half with broken-up polystyrene for drainage, to keep the overall weight down and make it easy to move from place to place. Look out for quirky items that aren't obvious containers at boot fairs or charity shops.

Top: Antirrhinums in a wicker basket.
Above: Vintage doll's pram with dianthus and sempervivums. **Opposite**: Bedding plants *Lantana* and yellow *Sanvitalia* 'Cuzco' in a plastic shopper.

perennial favourites

Just as you would use perennial plants and shrubs to form a long-lasting framework for a garden, you can do the same for your container display. As the pots will be their permanent home, you'll have to give them a bit more care and attention than when simply growing annuals that flower and die over the course of a year. Ideally, plant perennials in containers in the spring. I normally use a soil-based compost with up to 15 per cent grit added, to ensure the containers remain well drained in winter.

Some perennials may need to be staked. Do this in early May so that the plants can grow through the twigs or whatever support method you use and hide the supports. A fortnightly liquid feed with a potash-rich fertiliser such as tomato fertiliser will help keep them in good condition. Start in late April and continue until September. At the end of the year just leave the plants to die back naturally. In the spring, cut off any dead foliage and old flower spikes to about 10cm (4in) from the top of the pot. The plants should then start into growth again.

My favourites include aubrieta, ajuga and sweet violets in spring, followed later in the year by hollyhocks (these definitely need staking), frothy yellowy-green alchemilla (see page 145), various dwarf pinks and perennial wallflowers, all of which do perfectly well in pots.

Top: Lacehead hydrangea. **Above**: Perennial wallflower *Erysimum* 'Bowles's Mauve'. **Opposite**: A pink bush rose in an old bread tin.

A sunny sheltered position enclosed by walls, hedges, fences or shrubs will allow a shrub's fragrance to linger. It is also a much more pleasant place to sit and relax. I recommend spring-flowering daphnes – they have some of the best perfumes; *Viburnum* × *bodnantse* 'Dawn' does well in containers, as do some hydrangeas and roses (see pages 138 and 144).

Repotting

Perennials and shrubs will outgrow most containers every few years and exhaust the compost, so they will need to be repotted. A tell-tale sign is when the roots start growing out of the drainage holes. Repot in spring in a pot about one and a half times the size of the old one.

Ensure that the plant has been well watered the day before. If you cannot pull the plant out of its pot easily, take a bread knife, push it down the side of the pot and work your way round, loosening the compost and roots.

Remove the old compost on the surface of the plant and tease out the roots, cutting back any that have gone very woody. Just cut these back to the old rootball. Place some drainage material in the bottom of the pot, cover with a barrier (see page 34) and place about 8cm (3in) of fresh compost on top.

Position the old plant in the centre of the new container at its original depth and then trickle new compost down the gap between the rootball and the new container. Firm and water well. Leave a sufficient gap between the top of the compost and rim to allow you to mulch if necessary and to water well.

Above from top: Half-hardy fuchsias need winter protection; jasmine is the sort of plant that gives even a balcony a cottage-garden feel; bergamot is a scented hardy perennial beloved by bees. **Opposite:** Saxifrage is a hardy low-growing perennial.

container gardening for children

Giving children a packet of fast-growing seeds, some compost and a container is the best way to help them learn about where food and flowers come from. It's a good idea to begin with something as simple and speedy as mustard and cress on a sponge, so they can see results within 48 hours. Alternatively – or at the same time – sprinkle the seeds on a damp kitchen towel and place in a glass jar so they can see the roots and shoots develop. When the cress is ready the fun of making a sandwich with something they have grown will stay in the memory forever.

At the same time, plant some relatively slower-growing sunflower seeds, radishes and other plants with bright colours or memorable names; Bizzy Lizzies, Virginia stock and Black-eyed Susan are all favourites. Use crazy containers: nothing is off limits – colourful Wellingtons, buckets and plastic bins are all good – as long as they have drainage holes.

It's not easy to grow super-tall sunflowers in containers, but young gardeners can still compare height and sizes of the flower heads of the smaller varieties. And if a few children are involved, the competitive spirit is sure to prevail – keeping them interested. Encourage them to keep the dried sunflower heads to feed birds at the end of summer.

Above: You can help impatient youngsters by giving them plants already in flower to plant in novelty containers – a dianthus in a watering can, for example – to show off to friends and family. **Opposite, left**: *Helianthus annua* or sunflower – this is 'Ballard'. The newer dwarf varieties make fantastic container plants and will have the birds picking at the seeds at a height that can be enjoyed by children; **top right**: *Thunbergia alata* 'Superstar Orange' or Black-eyed Susan – what a stunner this is! Climbing up to 2m (6½ft) tall, it produces large orange flowers about the size of a 2p piece with a black centre; **bottom right**: Bright yellow dwarf coreopsis or tickseed is an easy flower for beginners, constantly flowering through July and August. This one is being planted in a plastic bucket with holes for drainage.

 Christine's tip

I was lucky enough to love gardening from a very early age and I used to sell my plants to neighbours. I did quite well... Now there's an incentive to get reluctant candidates interested!

contrasting combinations

Colourful annual bedding plants are fun to mix and match in containers – let your imagination run riot with wild and wonderful combinations. Bright yellow dwarf dahlias and hot pink trailing petunias can make a pleasant change from blue lobelia, white alyssum and red geraniums (although that's a favourite that will never go out of fashion).

Themed containers – either by colour, shape or style – are very satisfying. Cottage-garden lovers might like to try a traditional mix of tall blue delphiniums and low-growing pink dianthus; ultra modernists might like a mid-green yucca with complementary black or variegated grasses.

It is best to plant perennials in deeper containers as you want them to last for a few years, rather than one season (see pages 138 and 141 for more information). It's also best to invest in strong substantial pots – if buying terracotta pots, they need to be frostproof to withstand winter temperatures.

In my opinion it's the English roses which are grown in large (over 60cm/24in) terracotta pots that will delight you with their fragrance. Just ensure that they do not dry out and are grown in soil-based compost with good drainage, and feed with a good-quality rose fertiliser twice a year. I recommend 'Gertrude Jekyll' and 'Harlow Carr' with a contrasting underplanting of acid-green *Alchemilla mollis*.

Above: Gold, silver and bronze – a stainless steel colander is a suitable home for deep brown spikes of ornamental millet (this one is 'Purple Baron') with lovely dark foliage. This unusual crop is enhanced by stunning orange and bronze gazanias.
Opposite: A quintessentially English combination of old-fashioned pink roses and acid-green *Alchemilla mollis* turn an old metal tub into a mini country garden.

Christine's tip

Kitchen utensils such as colanders have built-in drainage holes and don't need moss or coir to line them, so make perfect containers and creative statements.

making
an impact

The advantage of container gardening is that you can move things about, create themes of colour or shape, rearrange the displays to bring the stars to the front and judiciously replace underperformers.

You can feed each plant the specialist nutrients it requires without affecting neighbouring plants and take risks by trying out exotic plants that need special attention. And when the high-summer flower show has died down, you can turn your hand to evergreens and topiary for dramatic interest. A balcony, terrace or small garden becomes your stage. So use it to make an impact.

unusual plants

PLANTS FOR TOPIARY

Box *Buxus sempervirens* – produces dark green glossy leaves, which clip well, forming a good dense habit. If fed and watered it is quick-growing.

Box-leaved honeysuckle *Lonicera nitida* – producing small dark green shiny leaves, this fast-growing dense evergreen makes an excellent topiary plant.

Privet *Ligustrum ovalifolium* – traditional hedging plant that clips so well, forming a good dense habit. The leaves are glossy, mid-green, and are evergreen in all but very severe winters.

Yew *Taxus baccata* – the leaves are flattened needles up to 3cm (1¼in) long with a pointed end. Yellow varieties are available.

Above: A simple box in Tuscan pot makes a big statement when little else is flowering.

Opposite: Simple topiary spheres and cones are created by careful trimming; complex spirals and animal shapes can be produced by training the young plant through a wire frame and clipping it as it grows to form dense growth in the shape of the frame.

architectural evergreen shrubs

Every garden needs structure and interest. The appealing foliage and shapes created by evergreens provide focal points and colour on a dull winter's day. They don't require high maintenance but remember that these leafy shrubs still need watering and feeding throughout the year – and are very prone to drying out during the winter. Dense foliage deflects the rain, so check *every* week to ensure that the compost is not bone-dry.

Evergreens take time before they show symptoms of drought and it can be as much as 4–6 months before the plant displays signs of stress and dies. This often happens during the summer and the gardener thinks the problem is current, when it could be that the plants were too dry over the previous winter.

Topiary

Topiary is the art of cutting evergreen shrubs into decorative shapes: box, yew, privet and bay look great when clipped into formal shapes.

 Christine's tip

I have found that any large tree or shrub is less likely to blow over if planted into a square container rather than a round one. This is particularly important if growing on a windy site. Bays tend to be top heavy, so plant in a square pot to prevent this problem.

designer colours

Evergreens don't have to be green. There are some superbly colourful plants that adapt well to container cultivation. Think of all the variegated evergreens, such as the many forms of euonymus, elaeagnus, the silver foliage of phlomis and santolina, the red new growth of photinia – they can all look great in a container on a cold winter's day.

More ways to add coloured foliage

Drought-tolerant sedums also come in a myriad of shades, from pink to orange to grey, and the leaf shapes are just as varied. Their fleshy leaves are efficient at storing and retaining water: the leaves' waxy tough outer coating makes the plants far less vulnerable to water loss by evaporation. Even the least green-fingered gardeners can have success with sedums. They can be left outside all year round – they are the ultimate low-maintenance plants.

The glorious plants opposite are perilla (sometimes called shiso), an edible herb from Japan that can grow up to 1m (3ft 3in) tall and have pink spikes of flowers in summer. They have been planted into a striking group of Indian cooking pots – with added drainage holes, of course. Perilla is a half-hardy annual, so seeds need to be started off under cover.

Top: A pink hardy geranium with trailing ornamental oregano in front.
Above: Fiery sedum in a concrete trough.
Opposite: Watch out for these varieties of perilla which look a little like coleus. Coleus (now correctly called *Solenostemon*) also have very beautiful colourful foliage but are not edible.

exotics

When you feel more confident, and you have a space indoors or a heated greenhouse to bring delicate plants inside in the winter, then it can be very exciting to grow some exotic plants. Even banana plants can be grown very successfully in containers. To get them to bear edible fruit is probably not practical – but still worth trying!

Easy species

Tropical plants such as alocasia with their arrow-shaped leaves, astelia which produce clumps of silver sword-like leaves, gingers with beautiful spikes of highly coloured flowers and the hedychiums are well worth trying to add an exotic look to your planting, and will thrive outside in a good summer. The vast majority of your large houseplants will also thrive outside during the summer and can add much to a tropical display – just don't forget to bring them back in again before the first frost and ensure that containers are well drained over the winter period. Most exotics will grow well in soil-based compost.

Exotic bulbs

Try crinum lilies in pink and white, spider lilies (*Hymenocallis* species), eucomis and cannas – those great brash tropical flowers that you often see as municipal bedding. They will overwinter under cover. Visitors will be scribbling notes and planning to grow some too.

wet and dry

So many of us would like a pond but don't have the space for one. Don't let that stop you from enjoying water plants: grow them in a container instead.

Fill a waterproof container such as a half-barrel or old tin bath with water (having cleaned it thoroughly beforehand). Gather together some compost suitable for aquatics, one or two 20cm (8in) lattice water-lily baskets, an old cotton pillow case, waterproof string, washed gravel, three or four bricks.

Line the lattice water-lily baskets with a square of old cotton – large enough to line the basket and allow you to bring the material up around the neck of the plant. Fill the lined baskets with aquatic compost. Plant the plants so that the compost is about 2cm (¾in) beneath the rim of the basket. Now tie the cotton square around the neck of the plant and cover with gravel until level with the rim of the basket and the fabric and knot are hidden. Water well. Position the bricks in the container then place the baskets on top, just under the water's surface.

Some like it hot

For a total contrast make a collection of drought lovers (see overleaf), including tall purple aeoniums, spiky agaves and mat-forming sempervivums, for a tactile and visual display.

Above: A tray of drought-loving sedums. Garden centres often sell ready-made collections like these.

why not try

WATER LOVERS

Acorus calamus 'Variegatus' – cream and green variegated leaves. When they first emerge in the early spring they are flushed with rose-pink, which fades with time. 1m (3ft 3in) tall.

Caltha palustris var. *alba* – the white flowering kingcup. Each flower may be up to 5cm (2in) across, produced above bright green foliage. Forms clumps up to 45cm (18in).

Iris laevigata – four mid-blue flowers are produced in early to mid-summer from each stem. The sword-shaped pale green leaves grow up to 60cm (24in) tall.

Nymphaea tetragona – white flowers no more than 5cm (2in) across float among oval or heart-shaped dark green leaves. It spreads to 25cm (10in). A charming miniature water lily.

show-stoppers

Lilies are highly fragrant and look great in different types of container, providing they are over 30cm (12in) in size. I love seeing half-barrels filled with lilies creating both colour and perfume. I grow them near my seating area in the garden – and by doors or windows so that their scent fills the house. I also love growing lilies for cut flowers and grow taller varieties in larger pots with long stems for arranging in vases. I leave the dwarf bulbs to bloom in containers so I can enjoy their flowers and fragrance in the garden. The varieties I think are really beautiful are listed on the right.

Planting lilies

Follow my instructions for a lovely display of lilies. Ensure the container is clean and has plenty of drainage holes. Place a layer of drainage material in the base and cover with a barrier layer. Fill the barrel to about a third of its depth with John Innes No. 2 compost, to which has been added 25 per cent grit. Cover this layer with 5cm (2in) of extra-sharp horticultural grit and place 10 lily bulbs on their sides evenly over the surface of the container as this allows water to drain through the scales and prevents rotting. Fill to the within 5cm (2in) of the top with the rest of the compost/grit mix. Mulch with a good layer of bark mulch. Water well. Depending on the varieties being used, plant either in the autumn or spring when the bulbs are available.

why not try

FRAGRANT ORIENTAL LILIES

The florist's favourite for bouquets, flowering July–September.

'Acapulco' – deep pink to red flowers. Height 90cm (36in).

'Anglia' – white with cerise half stripe in centre of petal that is spotted. Height 1.2m (4ft).

'Auratum Gold Band' – white with a gold band in the centre of the petals. Height 1.5m (5ft).

'Casa Blanca' – very large pure white flowers. Height 1.2m (4ft).

'Dizzy' – pale pink with bright red stripes. Height 1m (3ft 3in).

'Lombardia' – soft pure pink. Height 1–1.2m (3ft 3in–4ft).

 ## Christine's tip

When bringing lilies indoors, always remove the anthers from the flowers as their pollen can stain surfaces. If accidents occur lift the pollen with Sellotape. Do not attempt to wipe it off with a damp cloth as it will smear and stain.

Below: Elegant purple calla lilies.
Opposite: The fabulous beak- or claw-like
flowers of *Lotus berthelotii*. It's only half-
hardy so must be overwintered under cover.

Calla lilies (*Zantedeschia* species) include those striking lilies that come from Africa and are now available to grow here, producing white, purple, cream and green flowers with lance-shaped or narrow arrow-shaped foliage. They look fantastic growing in a container but must be overwintered in a warm greenhouse. They do best in a John Innes potting compost No. 2, fed every two weeks during the growing period with a potash-rich fertiliser. Stop feeding once they have flowered. Position in full sun in a sheltered site as winds will destroy the foliage.

Challenging plants

Growing unusual flowers can be a challenge. And challenges when overcome are very satisfying. If you have the time and the patience you will be rewarded if you have a go. My favourite 'challenging' plants are:

Devil's tongue (*Amorphophallus konjac*), an amazing aroid that in flower looks similar to the world-famous Titan lily but only growing to 1.3m (4ft 3in) tall and 1m (3ft 3in) wide with time. This plant produces a reddish-purple cowl-like flower up to 40cm (16in) long with a dark brown central protuberance. The smell when it flowers is awful!

Silk tree (*Albizia julibrissin*) produces lovely filigree foliage as a small tree with powder puff-like pink flowers – well, it does when grown somewhere really warm like Africa. I haven't managed it yet.

Lotus berthelotii is difficult to get to flower – buy young plants and grow them on and they'll flower in the second year. Its common names are parrot's beak or lobster claw and it produces trailing growths of silver leaves and masses of brilliant red and yellow flowers.

wildlife-friendly

plants to attract

BEES

Cone plants *Echinacea purpurea* – perennial. White to purple petals with an orange raised centre in late summer. Height 1m (3ft 3in).

Foxgloves *Digitalis purpurea* – biennial cottage-garden favourite of bees. Flower spikes up to 1.5m (5ft) tall.

Lavender *Lavandula* – perennial. 'Hidcote' is a safe bet for colour and fragrance.

BUTTERFLIES

Ice plant *Sedum spectabile* – perennial. A succulent plant producing pink flowers through the summer.

Lavender – see above.

Red valerian *Centranthus ruber* – perennial. Clusters of red flowers June–October.

Sweet rocket *Hesperis matronalis* – perennial. White, violet or purple flowers, highly scented in the evening from May to August.

HOVERFLIES

Pot marigolds *Calendula officinalis* – lovely hardy, easy-to-grow annual with daisy-like orange flowers. Height 30cm (12in).

Toadflax *Linaria vulgaris* – delightful annual with spikes of yellow. Height 45cm (18in).

MOTHS

Evening primrose *Oenothera biennis* – hardy biennial producing fragrant yellow flowers April to July. Height up to 1m (3ft 3in).

Tobacco plant *Nicotiana alata* – clear white evening scented flowers are produced on this tall sticky plant mid-summer to mid-autumn. Height 1m (3ft 3in).

Gardening connects you to nature and the seasons and one of the nicest aspects of having a garden is the amount of wildlife that it attracts. Anything you can do to encourage insects and bees is going to help the terrible reduction in population of the pollinating creatures that are necessary to our survival, so do plant with this in mind.

Do not despair if you do not have a large garden as even on a patio or in a window box you can do a lot to attract wildlife into your outdoor space. I have lots of containers around my garden for this purpose and I just love hearing the bees working the flowers and watching the butterflies during the summer.

We need butterflies, moths, bees and hoverflies to pollinate flowers and fruit. Lavender, perennial sedum, red valerian, marigolds and, of course, buddleja will bring these winged insects to your pots and window boxes.

Ladybirds will eat the greenfly from your rose bushes. All birds love sunflower seeds: grow them to attract robins and they'll snack on the grubs in the soil and blue tits will peck at the caterpillars.

Above left: Buddleja davidii is known as the 'Butterfly Bush'. This perennial shrub produces cone-shaped flowers in purple, white, pink or red. Often hundreds of butterflies will cover the shrub. It can grow very tall, so trim back hard after flowering. Deadheading the flowers will result in a longer display. *Opposite:* The flowers of *Butomus*, an aquatic plant, prove irresistible to bees.

ferns

If you have a period house with one of those shady bits at the back then why not do what a vast number of Victorians did in the 19th century and create a fernery? Pteridomania is the name for the craze that gripped the nation for about 30 years and people vied with each other to collect unusual ferns. You can display a collection of ferns on a recycled metal shelf unit or make staging from items from the junk shop.

Ferns are our oldest known plant and come in many forms, from feathery maidenhairs to the shiny bird's nests with their beautiful green leaves. Each has a beauty of its own and when you get going the attraction will become clear. There are ferns for dry places and also for damp situations so check before buying, to ensure you have the right type for your own situation. Frogs and toads like to use the fronds for cover. You will need to plant in humus-rich, moist but well-drained soil, which has up to 20 per cent grit added. Placing a saucer under the pot in the height of summer will help to keep the soil moist. Never let them dry out but in winter they need to be well drained – sitting in water will cause them to rot.

Want some ideas?

If you need inspiration, the Chelsea Physic Garden in London has a very fine example of a fernery that has been there for more than a hundred years.

Top: A modern-day fernery. **Above**: The head or crozier of a fern as it unfurls in spring – an image that has inspired many painters and photographers. **Opposite**: A soft shield fern in an antique lead gutter head.

why not try

Bird's nest fern *Asplenium nidus* – commonly grown slow-growing evergreen.

Hen and chicken fern *Asplenium bulbiferum*.

Lady fern or common lady fern *Athyrium filix-femina*.

Silver-dollar fern or Peruvian maidenhair *Adiantum peruvianum*.

Soft shield fern *Polystichum setiferum* – evergreen and hardy.

olives

Growing an olive tree in a container is a positive advantage in many areas of the UK as it means you can bring it under cover when the temperature drops. Of course, you'll have to keep it in a manageable-sized pot, preferably one that you can manoeuvre on to a trolley or into a wheelbarrow. In mild parts of the UK you can leave the tree outside, but protect it by covering with horticultural fleece. Also wrap the container in bubble wrap to stop the soil from freezing. In colder parts of the UK bring the plant into a warm greenhouse. Let's face it, though, it's probably best to grow an olive tree for its silvery foliage and gnarled trunk, as you're unlikely to get a significant harvest.

Planting

Add sufficient drainage to the base of the pot – a 10–15cm (4–6in) layer should be enough. I use John Innes potting compost No. 2 but I mix in an additional 20 per cent of horticultural grit.

'Aglandau' is the hardiest of the varieties currently available and is self-fertile; 'Cailletier' is fairly hardy and self-fertile; 'Sativa' has small white, scented flowers in late spring and summer; 'Frantoio' is a popular Italian variety.

Above: This true olive, *Olea europaea*, has been bonsai-pruned and its roots restricted to keep it small. It's a bit of a one-off but you should be able to order one from a specialist nursery.
Opposite: A full-sized tree.

Overleaf: Builders' bags with phacelia, often sown as a green manure – when it's chopped down and dug in to improve the soil. It's also wildlife-friendly – bees love the flowers.

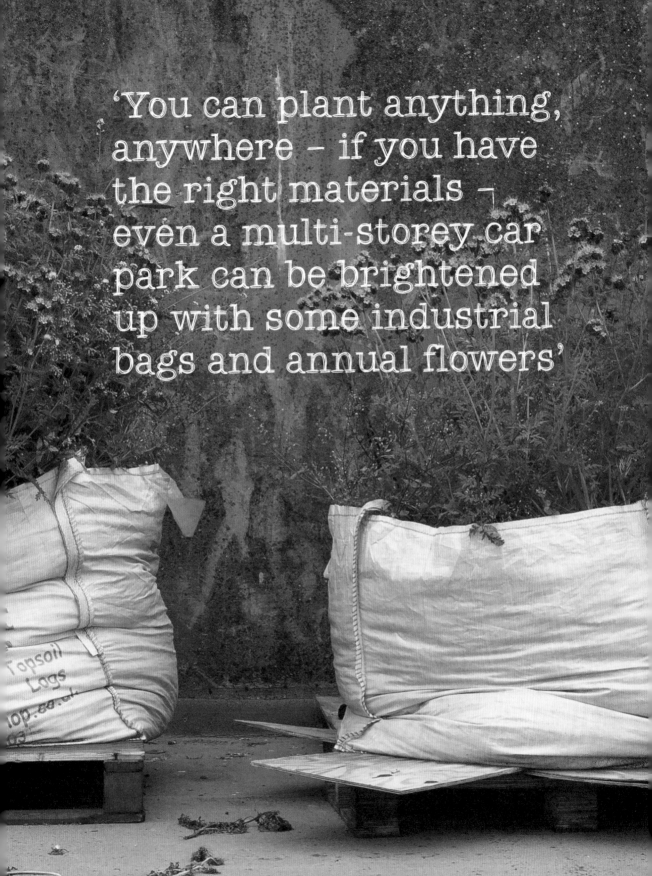

'You can plant anything, anywhere – if you have the right materials – even a multi-storey car park can be brightened up with some industrial bags and annual flowers'

index

Note: Page numbers in **bold** indicate major sections.